PreK-
K

Letter Dot-to-Dot

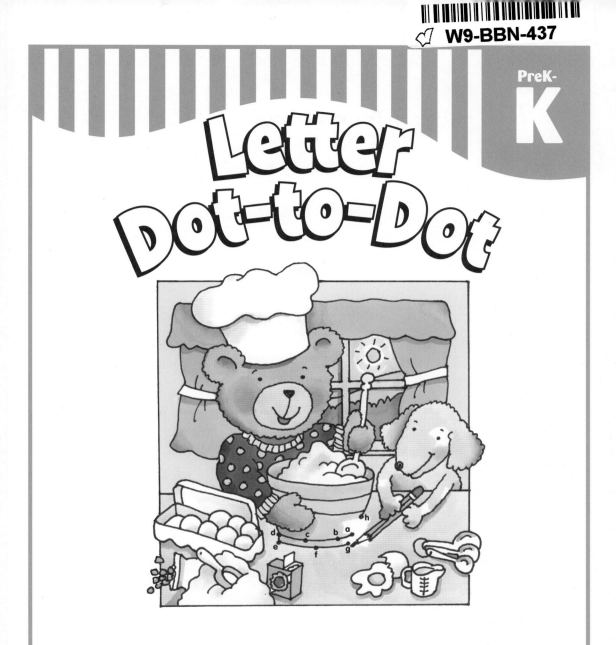

Written by Hanna Otero

Illustrations by Creston Ely

FlashKids
New York

This book belongs to

_____

New York

An Imprint of Sterling Publishing
387 Park Avenue South
New York, NY 10016

FLASH KIDS, STERLING, and the distinctive Sterling logo are registered trademarks of
Sterling Publishing Co., Inc.

Text and illustrations © 2006 by Flash Kids

Cover design and production by Mada Design, Inc.

ISBN 978-1-4114-3462-2

Distributed in Canada by Sterling Publishing
c/o Canadian Manda Group, 165 Dufferin Street
Toronto, Ontario, Canada M6K 3H6
Distributed in the United Kingdom by GMC Distribution Services
Castle Place, 166 High Street, Lewes, East Sussex, England BN7 1XU
Distributed in Australia by Capricorn Link (Australia) Pty. Ltd.
P.O. Box 704, Windsor, NSW 2756, Australia

For information about custom editions, special sales, and premium and
corporate purchases, please contact Sterling Special Sales
at 800-805-5489 or specialsales@sterlingpublishing.com.

Manufactured in China

Lot #:
8 10 9 7
05/12

www.flashkids.com

Dear Parent,

The alphabet is an important first step on the road to reading. *Letter Dot-to-Dot* will help your child master both uppercase and lowercase letters. By connecting the dots in each picture, your child is building essential alphabetizing skills, with emphasis on every letter from A to Z! To get the most from *Letter Dot-to-Dot*, follow these simple steps:

- Find a comfortable place where you and your child can work quietly together.
- Encourage your child to go at his or her own pace.
- Help your child sound out the letters and identify the pictures.
- Offer lots of praise and support.
- Let your child reward his or her work with the included stickers.
- Most of all, remember that learning should be fun! Take time to color the pictures, laugh at the funny characters, and enjoy this special time spent together.

Good morning!

Connect the dots from **A** to **F**.
Color the picture.

I wake up.

Connect the dots from **A** to **G**.
Color the picture.

Tabby is still sleeping.

Connect the dots from **A** to **H**.
Color the picture.

Mom is awake.

Connect the dots from **A** to **I**.
Color the picture.

Dad will make breakfast.

Connect the dots from **A** to **J**.
Color the picture.

I can help Dad cook.

Connect the dots from **A** to **K**.
Color the picture.

We need a bowl.

Connect the dots from **A** to **L**.
Color the picture.

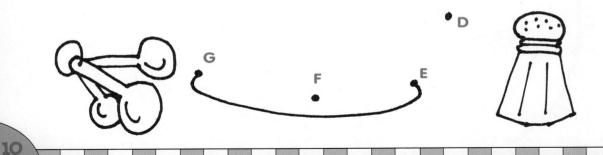

We need a whisk.

Connect the dots from **A** to **M**.

Color the picture.

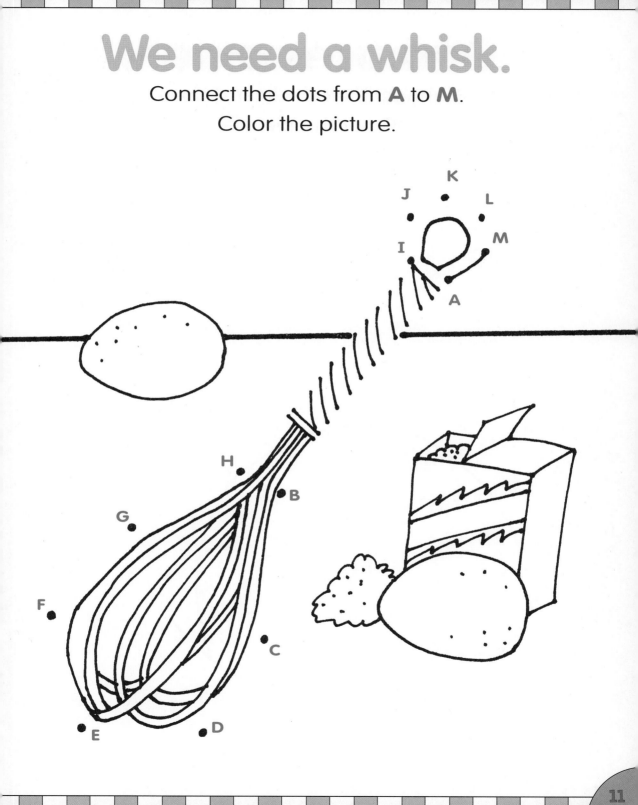

Dad uses a pan.

Connect the dots from **A** to **N**.
Color the picture.

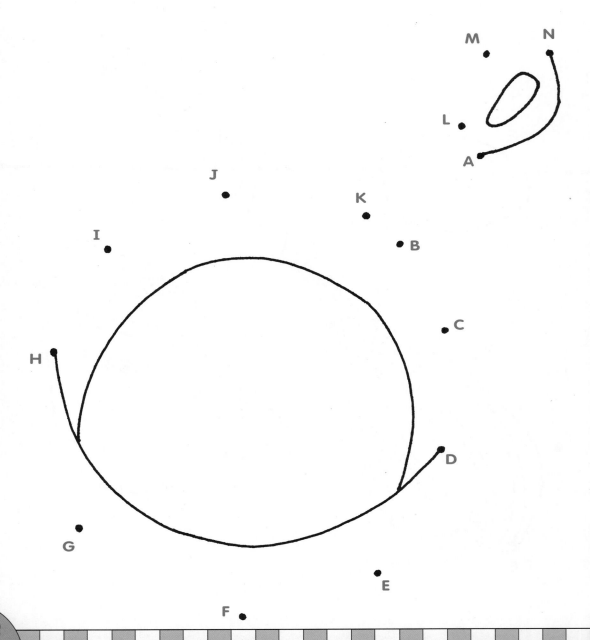

He uses a spatula too.

Connect the dots from **A** to **O**.
Color the picture.

I like to watch Dad cook.

Connect the dots from **A** to **P**.

Color the picture.

Pancakes smell good.

Connect the dots from **A** to **Q**.
Color the picture.

I get bacon from the refrigerator.

Connect the dots from **A** to **R**.

Color the picture.

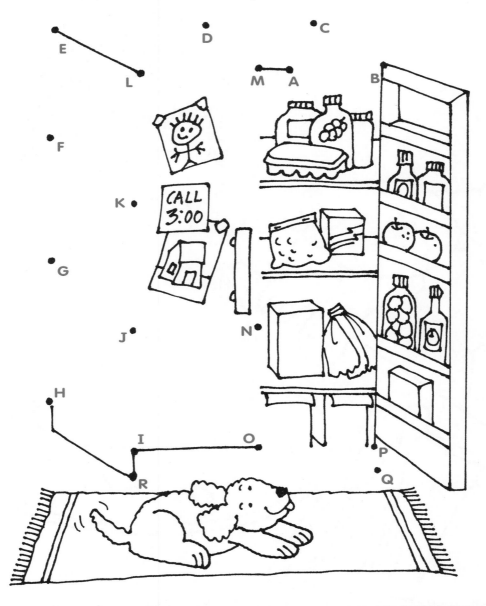

We cook it in the pan.

Connect the dots from **A** to **S**.

Color the picture.

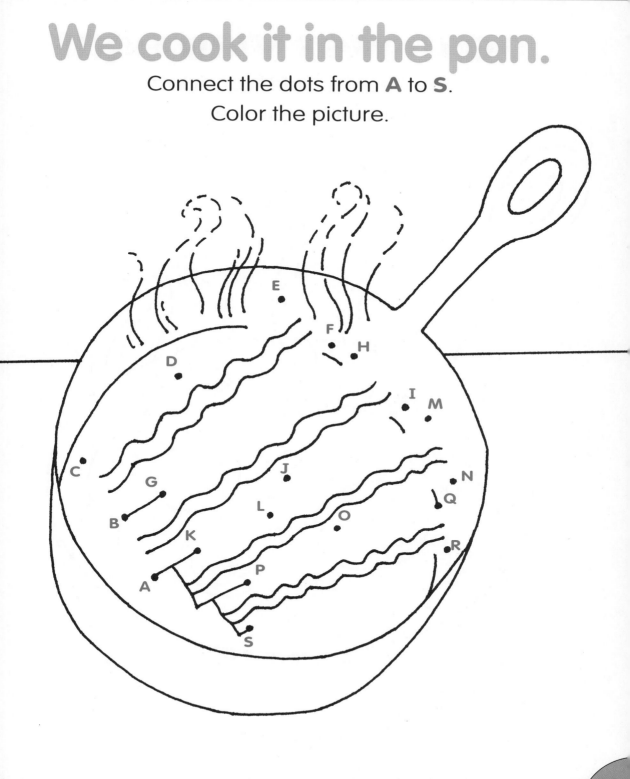

Dad makes fried eggs.

Connect the dots from **A** to **T**.

Color the picture.

Mom sets the table.

Connect the dots from **A** to **U**.

Color the picture.

I carry the dishes carefully.

Connect the dots from **A** to **V**.
Color the picture.

I get the milk.

Connect the dots from **A** to **W**.
Color the picture.

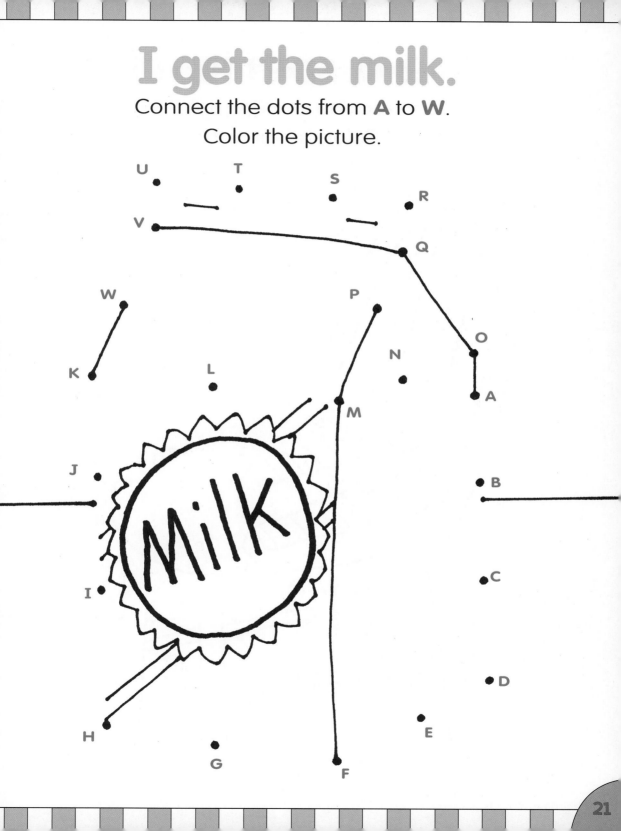

I have a special chair.

Connect the dots from **A** to **X**.
Color the picture.

Tabby sits under me.

Connect the dots from **A** to **Y**.
Color the picture.

I drink milk.

Connect the dots from **A** to **Z**.
Color the picture.

I eat lots of pancakes.

Connect the dots from **A** to **Z**.
Color the picture.

We wash the dishes.

Connect the dots from **A** to **Z**.
Color the picture.

Now Mom helps me brush my teeth.

Connect the dots from **A** to **Z**.
Color the picture.

Time for a bath!

Connect the dots from **E** to **N**.
Color the picture.

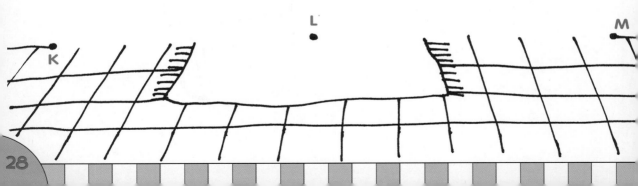

I make room for my bath toys.

Connect the dots from **G** to **P**.

Color the picture.

After my bath,
I comb my hair.

Connect the dots from **J** to **S**.
Color the picture.

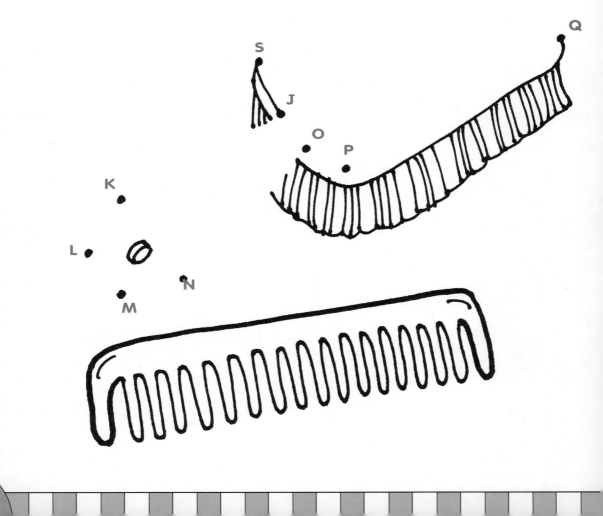

I look and feel clean.

Connect the dots from **Q** to **Z**.
Color the picture.

I get dressed.

Connect the dots from **B** to **K**.
Color the picture.

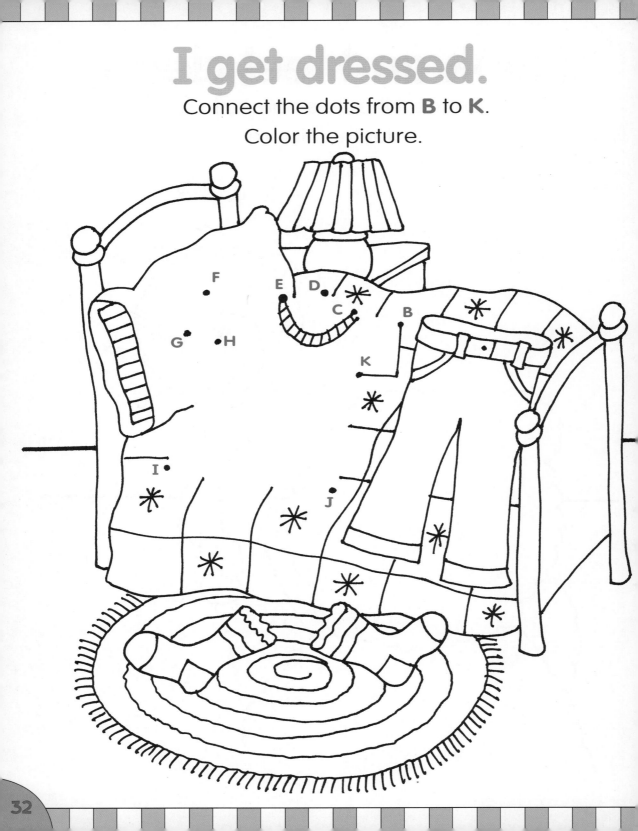

I am ready to play.

Connect the dots from **H** to **Q**.
Color the picture.

This is my playhouse.

Connect the dots from **a** to **e**.
Color the picture.

I like the swing set.

Connect the dots from **a** to **f**.

Color the picture.

The slide is my favorite.

Connect the dots from **a** to **g**.
Color the picture.

I can ride my bike.

Connect the dots from **a** to **h**.

Color the picture.

I can pull my wagon.

Connect the dots from **a** to **i**.

Color the picture.

Time for lunch!

Connect the dots from **a** to **j**.
Color the picture.

Mom makes a big sandwich.

Connect the dots from **a** to **k**.
Color the picture.

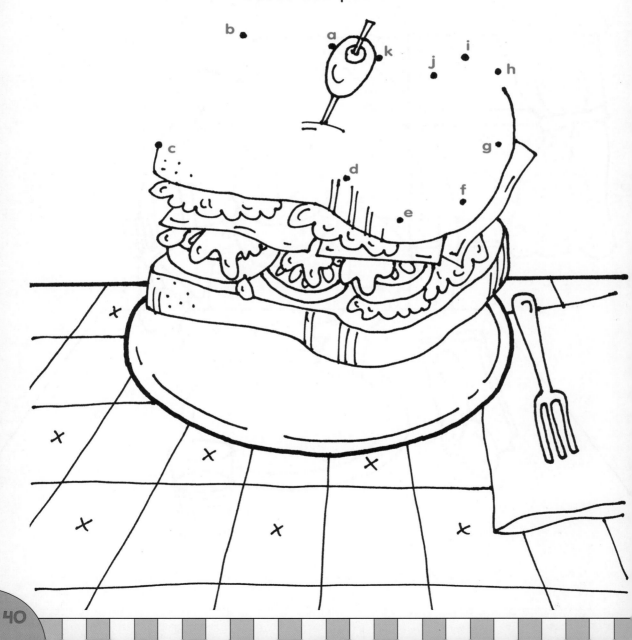

I eat carrots.

Connect the dots from **a** to **l**.
Color the picture.

This is Lucky's lunch.

Connect the dots from **a** to **m**.
Color the picture.

After lunch, I take a nap.

Connect the dots from **a** to **n**.
Color the picture.

g

h

f

i

e

j

d

k

c b

m l

a

n

When I wake up, we go to town.

Connect the dots from **a** to **o**.

Color the picture.

j

k

l

i

h

a

b

g

c

d
e
f

m

o

n

We go shopping.

Connect the dots from **a** to **p**.

Color the picture.

Mom pays for the food.

Connect the dots from **a** to **q**.

Color the picture.

I help carry the bags.

Connect the dots from **a** to **r**.

Color the picture.

We go to the post office.

Connect the dots from **a** to **s**.

Color the picture.

We see the mail truck.

Connect the dots from **a** to **t**.
Color the picture.

We mail a letter.

Connect the dots from **a** to **u**.
Color the picture.

50

I put it in the mailbox.

Connect the dots from **a** to **v**.
Color the picture.

At home, we do the laundry.

Connect the dots from **a** to **w**.

Color the picture.

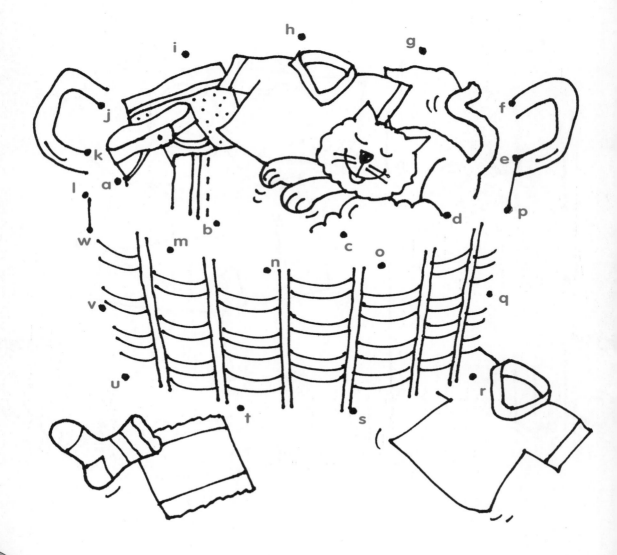

I watch the clothes dry.

Connect the dots from **a** to **x**.
Color the picture.

We fold the clothes.

Connect the dots from **a** to **y**.

Color the picture.

I wash my hands for dinner.

Connect the dots from **a** to **z**.
Color the picture.

We eat spaghetti.

Connect the dots from **a** to **z**.

Color the picture.

We have salad too.

Connect the dots from **a** to **z**.
Color the picture.

After dinner,
Dad and I build a fort.

Connect the dots from **d** to **m**.

Color the picture.

We all read a story.

Connect the dots from **f** to **o**.
Color the picture.

I put on my pajamas.

Connect the dots from **i** to **r**.

Color the picture.

Lucky is ready for bed.

Connect the dots from **l** to **u**.
Color the picture.

Tabby is ready too.

Connect the dots from **o** to **x**.
Color the picture.

Good night!

Connect the dots from **c** to **l**.
Color the picture.

You connected the dots and finished the story.

Great Job!

_____,
(Name)

now you know your ABCs!

AWESOME!

U.S.MAIL

Milk

Flash Kids
LEARNING IN A FLASH

Great Job!